Alex Latimer

Introduction

Lots of English words can be **tricky to spell** – some of them have **silent letters**, some **break the rules** about how words are usually spelled, and many **aren't spelled as they sound**. For example, the "**g**" sound can be spelled "**g**" in "gate", "**gg**" in "egg", "**gh**" in "ghost" and "**gu**" in "guest".

The only way to spell these words correctly is to **put in some practice and learn** each one. This can seem like a lot of work, but it's **not as hard as you think**.

If you learn **a few new words each day**, you'll be surprised how quickly you feel more confident about your spelling. **This book will help you to do that**.

You'll find **300 tricky words** in this book, and space to **test yourself** on them. To help you learn, the words are in groups of three, and each group has something in common. For example, "**rhyme**", "**rhythm**" and "**rhinoceros**" all have an unexpected "**h**" after the "**r**".

At the back of the book there are some useful **spelling rules and tips**, along with a **checklist of all 300 words** so you can tick them off when you've learned them.

There are plenty of other ways to make learning spelling fun. You'll find some ideas for **spelling games, spelling puzzles and spelling quizzes** as well as lots more spelling **hints and tips**, at the Usborne Quicklinks website.

Go to:

www.usborne.com/quicklinks

and type the keywords "**read and write**", then click on "**Young readers**".

How to use this book

One good way to use this book is with the spelling method called:

Look Say Cover Write Check

Here's how to do it:

Look at the first word on a page, then **say** it to yourself and try to remember how to spell it. Now **cover** up the word, and **write** it next to the number 1, then **check** if you've got it right. You've got space to write each word **three times**, in case you get it wrong at first.

Then do the same five steps with the second and third words. **Use a pencil** so you can **rub out if you go wrong**.

1 science

2 conscious

3 conscience

1

2

3

1 **knock**

2 **knuckle**

3 **knight**

---

1 Knock

2 Knuckle

3 Knight

1   rhyme

2   rhythm

3   rhinoceros

1

2

3

---

1 Wednesday

2 handsome

3 handkerchief

1 _____

_____

_____

2 _____

_____

_____

3 _____

_____

8

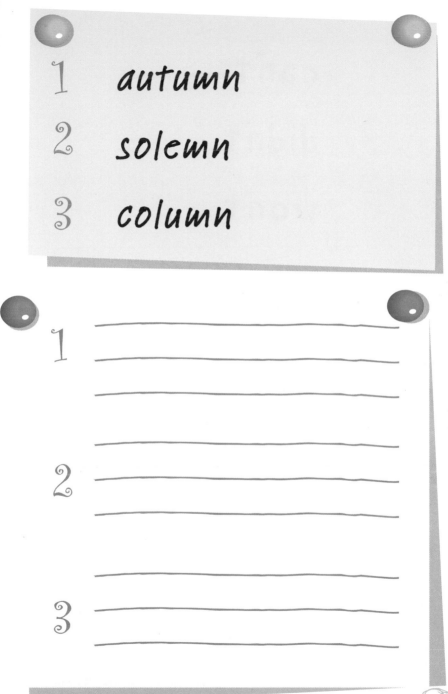

1 *autumn*

2 *solemn*

3 *column*

1

2

3

1 can't

2 didn't

3 won't

_____

1

_____

2

_____

3

_____

1 whale

2 which

3 rhubarb

1

2

3

1 receive

2 deceive

3 ceiling

1

2

3

1 mischievous

2 thieves

3 believe

1 *happiness*

2 *appetite*

3 *disappear*

1

2

3

1 height

2 weight

3 eight

1

2

3

1   wrong

2   written

3   wrist

1

2

3

1 parliament

2 marriage

3 miniature

1

2

3

1 medieval

2 ancient

3 glacier

1

2

3

1   numb

2   thumb

3   crumb

1

2

3

1   recycle

2   bicycle

3   cygnet

1   ------------------

2   ------------------

3   ------------------

1   tickle

2   chuckle

3   unlucky

---

1 _____

---

2 _____

---

3 _____

1. children

2. exchange

3. sandwich

1.

2.

3.

1 pleasant

2 breakfast

3 already

1 _____

2 _____

3 _____

1 beautiful

2 colleague

3 meanwhile

1

2

3

1 weary

2 earn

3 heart

1

2

3

1 ocean

2 earth

3 heaven

_____

1

_____

2

_____

3

_____

1 **fought**

2 **bought**

3 **brought**

1

2

3

1 friend

2 fierce

3 quiet

1 _____
_____
_____

2 _____
_____
_____

3 _____
_____
_____

1 *disconnect*

2 *anniversary*

3 *annual*

1 _____
_____
_____

2 _____
_____
_____

3 _____
_____
_____

1 previous

2 obvious

3 curious

1

2

3

1 committee

2 accommodation

3 recommend

1

2

3

1 apprentice

2 hippopotamus

3 appalled

1

2

3

1 occasionally

2 broccoli

3 occurred

1

2

3

1   *bright*

2   *frightening*

3   *lightning*

1

2

3

1 *autograph*

2 *telephone*

3 *autobiography*

1

2

3

1 photograph

2 pharaoh

3 sphere

1

2

3

1   professor

2   profession

3   profit

1

2

3

1 business

2 across

3 guess

1

2

3

1 actually

2 normally

3 really

1

2

3

1   emotion

2   attention

3   traditional

1

2

3

1   dictionary

2   national

3   audition

1

2

3

1. education
2. ambition
3. qualification

1.

2.

3.

1. pronunciation

2. translation

3. revolution

1.

2.

3.

1 competition

2 pollution

3 description

1

2

3

1 decision

2 explosion

3 television

1

2

3

1. **quickly**

2. **pocket**

3. **o'clock**

1.

2.

3.

1 **tomorrow**

2 **embarrassing**

3 **interrupt**

1

2

3

---

1 *horror*

2 *terror*

3 *corridor*

1 _____
_____
_____

2 _____
_____
_____

3 _____
_____
_____

1   *difference*
2   *official*
3   *traffic*

1   _____
    _____
    _____

2   _____
    _____
    _____

3   _____
    _____
    _____

1 politician

2 optician

3 magician

1

2

3

1   **thought**

2   **thorough**

3   **through**

1

2

3

1 because

2 sausage

3 trauma

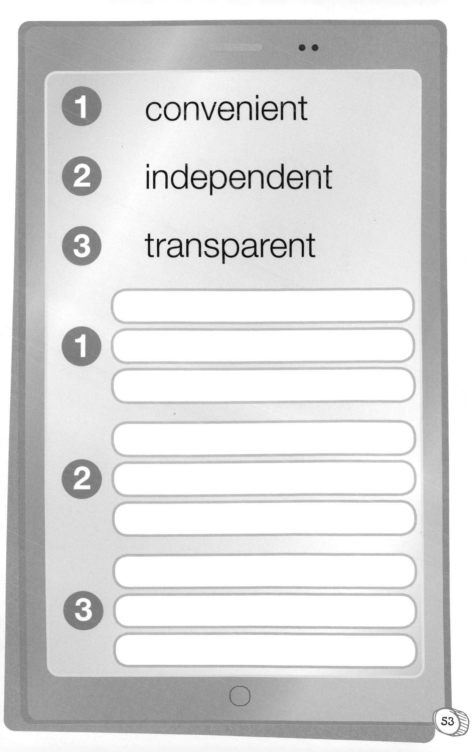

1 convenient

2 independent

3 transparent

1   yacht

2   anchor

3   attached

1

2

3

1 *should*

2 *would*

3 *could*

1

2

3

1   celebrity

2   cemetery

3   excited

1

2

3

1 precious

2 delicious

3 vicious

1

2

3

1 glamorous

2 humorous

3 cautious

1

2

3

1 citizen

2 circus

3 circle

1

2

3

1 wound

2 journey

3 mourn

1 _____

2 _____

3 _____

1 playful

2 grateful

3 successful

1 _____

2 _____

3 _____

1 icicle

2 cubicle

3 article

1

2

3

1   expensive

2   relative

3   aggressive

_____

1   _____

2   _____

3   _____

1 **trouble**

2 **grumble**

3 **double**

1

2

3

1   crumple

2   example

3   dimple

1

2

3

1 specific

2 prehistoric

3 organic

1

2

3

1   reliable

2   miserable

3   valuable

1

2

3

1 receipt

2 cupboard

3 raspberry

1 _____

2 _____

3 _____

1 responsible

2 sensible

3 impossible

1

2

3

1. chalk

2. folk

3. yolk

1.

2.

3.

1. igloo
2. school
3. balloon

_____

1.

_____

2.

_____

3.

_____

1 scene

2 scissors

3 scent

1

2

3

1. doubt

2. debt

3. comb

1.
   - [ ]
   - [ ]
   - [ ]

2.
   - [ ]
   - [ ]
   - [ ]

3.
   - [ ]
   - [ ]
   - [ ]

1 *cough*

2 *enough*

3 *rough*

1

2

3

1 *nephew*

2 *phantom*

3 *phrase*

1

2

3

1 ghastly

2 ghost

3 ghoul

1

2

3

1   foreign

2   sign

3   design

1

2

3

1 whiskers

2 whisper

3 white

1

2

3

1 unique

2 squirrel

3 conqueror

1

2

3

1 baggage

2 damage

3 image

---

1 _____

2 _____

3 _____

1   hedgehog

2   knowledge

3   fidget

1

2

3

1. accident

2. accent

3. access

1.

2.

3.

1. Occupy
2. Soccer
3. Morocco

1.

2.

3.

1 accelerate

2 desperate

3 exaggerate

1

2

3

1 chaos

2 echo

3 character

1

2

3

1   guitar

2   spectacular

3   separate

1

2

3

1   entertainment

2   environment

3   government

1

2

3

1 giant

2 ginger

3 giraffe

1 _____
_____
_____

2 _____
_____
_____

3 _____
_____

1 gentle

2 gypsy

3 gerbil

1 _____
_____
_____

2 _____
_____
_____

3 _____
_____
_____

1) definite

2) invite

3) polite

1)

2)

3)

1. muscle

2. adolescent

3. discipline

1.

2.

3.

1 emergency

2 fancy

3 literacy

1

2

3

1 recipe

2 necessary

3 especially

1 college

2 privilege

3 siege

1

2

3

1   asthma

2   castle

3   whistle

1

2

3

1 island

2 debris

3 aisle

1

2

3

1 February

2 library

3 comfortable

1

2

3

1 half

2 calm

3 calf

1

2

3

1   swerve

2   sword

3   answer

1

2

3

1   almond

2   salmon

3   colonel

---

1   _ _ _ _ _ _ _ _ _ _ _

2   _ _ _ _ _ _ _ _ _ _ _

3   _ _ _ _ _ _ _ _ _ _ _

1 slaughter

2 naughty

3 daughter

1 - - - - - - - - - - - - -
- - - - - - - - - - - - -
- - - - - - - - - - - - -

2 - - - - - - - - - - - - -
- - - - - - - - - - - - -
- - - - - - - - - - - - -

3 - - - - - - - - - - - - -
- - - - - - - - - - - - -
- - - - - - - - - - - - -

1 leopard

2 people

3 geography

_____

1

_____

2

_____

3

_____

1. neither

2. heir

3. weird

_____

1. _____

2. _____

3. _____

1   sieve

2   achieve

3   niece

1

2

3

Spelling tips

Here are some **tips to help you improve your spelling**. Different approaches work better for different people, so try out a few of these ideas to find the ones that are best for you.

Learn words in groups

It often helps to remember **pairs of words** or **groups of words** that are **spelled in a similar way**, like each group of three words in this book. As you move on to new words, you can divide them into groups yourself.

Helpful phrases

Try **making up little phrases** to remind you how to spell words that you find especially difficult. For example, to remember "**necessary**" you could say, "A shirt has one **c**ollar and two **s**leeves." This reminds you that necessary has one "**c**" and two "**s**"s. This can be very useful when trying to remember how to spell longer words.

Break words into chunks

It's helpful to break some tricky words down into **short sections**:

Wednesday = Wed - nes - day
business = bus - in - ess

It's sometimes a lot easier to remember these little chunks than to try to remember a whole word.

Create a funny sentence

It can be fun, and also very useful, to **make up a sentence using all the letters in the word in order**. For example, to remember "**rhythm**" you can say: "**r**hythm **h**elps **y**our **t**wo **h**ips **m**ove". The sillier you can make the sentence, the more likely you are to remember it. Here are a couple more:

because:
big **e**lephants **c**an't **a**lways **u**se **s**mall **e**xits

quiet:
queens' **u**nderwear **is** **e**xtremely **t**ight

Think of a picture

It can help to **imagine an unusual picture** to help you spell a word. For example, "**a limo with a mouse in**" might remind you how to spell the word "**limousine**".

Say it out loud

Sometimes you might find a word hard to spell because you're not saying it correctly. Although many words are not spelled the way they sound, **it's hard to spell a word if you are picturing it wrong in your head**. For example, you might be saying "spectaclar" instead of "spectac_u_lar". Try **reading the word slowly and saying it out loud** at the same time to avoid any mistakes.

Make a list of tricky words

On pages 109-112 you'll find a **list of all the tricky words** to spell in this book so you can keep track of your progress. But you could also make your own list of words, adding any word that you struggle with so you can work on it.

A few spelling rules

A lot of the words in this book don't follow any spelling rules. But there are a few rules that are almost always right and these are worth knowing:

1. In English, the letter "**q**" is always followed by the letter "**u**".

2. English words **never start with the same consonant twice**. (Consonants are all the letters apart from "**a**", "**e**", "**i**", "**o**" and "**u**", which are the vowels.) So you won't find a word that begins "**ss**" or "**tt**" or "**pp**".

3. The letters "**j**" and "**v**" are always followed by a vowel (or a "**y**").

4. The letters "**h**", "**j**", "**k**", "**q**", "**v**", "**w**", "**x**" and "**y**" are **never used twice in a row** in any English words.

Rules like this can help you a little, but there's only one rule really: the best way to learn is by putting in as much practice as you can. Good luck!

Checklist

This checklist contains all 300 tricky words from this book, in the same order as they appear in the book. As you work through the book you can keep track of your progress – once you've learned to spell a word, you can tick it off the list.

science
conscious
conscience
knock
knuckle
knight
rhyme
rhythm
rhinoceros
Wednesday
handsome
handkerchief
autumn
solemn
column
can't
didn't
won't
whale
which

rhubarb
receive
deceive
ceiling
mischievous
thieves
believe
happiness
appetite
disappear
height
weight
eight
wrong
written
wrist
parliament
marriage
miniature
medieval

ancient
glacier
numb
thumb
crumb
recycle
bicycle
cygnet
tickle
chuckle
unlucky
children
exchange
sandwich
pleasant
breakfast
already
beautiful
colleague
meanwhile

weary
earn
heart
ocean
earth
heaven
fought
bought
brought
friend
fierce
quiet
disconnect
anniversary
annual
previous
obvious
curious
committee
accommodation
recommend
apprentice
hippopotamus
appalled
occasionally
broccoli
occurred
bright
frightening
lightning

autograph
telephone
autobiography
photograph
pharaoh
sphere
professor
profession
profit
business
across
guess
actually
normally
really
emotion
attention
traditional
dictionary
national
audition
education
ambition
qualification
pronunciation
translation
revolution
competition
pollution
description

decision
explosion
television
quickly
pocket
o'clock
tomorrow
embarrassing
interrupt
horror
terror
corridor
difference
official
traffic
politician
optician
magician
thought
thorough
through
because
sausage
trauma
convenient
independent
transparent
yacht
anchor
attached

should
would
could
celebrity
cemetery
excited
precious
delicious
vicious
glamorous
humorous
cautious
citizen
circus
circle
wound
journey
mourn
playful
grateful
successful
icicle
cubicle
article
expensive
relative
aggressive
trouble
grumble
double

crumple
example
dimple
specific
prehistoric
organic
reliable
miserable
valuable
receipt
cupboard
raspberry
responsible
sensible
impossible
chalk
folk
yolk
igloo
school
balloon
scene
scissors
scent
doubt
debt
comb
cough
enough
rough

nephew
phantom
phrase
ghastly
ghost
ghoul
foreign
sign
design
whiskers
whisper
white
unique
squirrel
conqueror
baggage
damage
image
hedgehog
knowledge
fidget
accident
accent
access
occupy
soccer
Morocco
accelerate
desperate
exaggerate

chaos	asthma
echo	castle
character	whistle
guitar	island
spectacular	debris
separate	aisle
entertainment	February
environment	library
government	comfortable
giant	half
ginger	calm
giraffe	calf
gentle	swerve
gypsy	sword
gerbil	answer
definite	almond
invite	salmon
polite	colonel
muscle	slaughter
adolescent	naughty
discipline	daughter
emergency	leopard
fancy	people
literacy	geography
recipe	neither
necessary	heir
especially	weird
college	sieve
privilege	achieve
siege	niece